A CHRISTIAN'S POCKET GUIDE TO

JESUS CHRIST

Those who get a glimpse of Christ's glory are astonished. People can descend 35,000 feet below the sea into the Marianas Trench, but our skill fails us when we probe the depths of Christ's person and work. But faith seeks understanding, and love wants to know its Beloved. Mark Jones has served us well by writing this short introduction to the doctrine of Christ. His book is biblical, clear, and rooted in historic Reformed theology. It is an excellent tool for personal study or for classes in church or school.

JOEL R. BEEKE,
President, Puritan Reformed Theological Seminary,
Grand Rapids, Michigan

Who is Jesus Christ? Our answer to that question will determine our eternity. What we believe *about* Jesus is essential to our belief *in* Jesus. In this book, Dr. Mark Jones helps to answer hard questions about the person and work of Jesus Christ in a simple and clear manner. This book is an excellent tool for evangelism and discipleship, and it is a much-needed resource for new believers, laypeople, and pastors alike.

Burk Parsons,
Associate Pastor, Saint Andrew's Chapel, Sanford, Florida.
Editor of *Tabletalk* magazine

A CHRISTIAN'S POCKET GUIDE TO

JESUS CHRIST

AN INTRODUCTION TO CHRISTOLOGY

MARK JONES

Copyright © Mark Jones 2012

ISBN 978-1-84550-951-4 – Book
ISBN 978-1-78191-091-7 – ePub
ISBN 978-1-78191-095-5 – Mobi

Published in 2012 and reprinted in 2017
by
Christian Focus Publications Ltd,
Geanies House, Fearn, Ross-shire,
IV20 1TW, Scotland, Great Britain
www.christianfocus.com

Cover design by Paul Lewis

Printed and bound by Nørhaven, Denmark

CONTENTS

⚠ Warning
🖉 Don't Forget
⑦ Stop and Think
⚹ Point of Interest

PREFACE

The topic of Christology concerns the person and work of Jesus Christ, the God-man (*theanthropos*). In theology, Christology has an importance that cannot be overstated. Christ's person and work are the central point of Christian theology. Yet we are far more comfortable discussing his work (what he did), than we are understanding his person (who he is). This is understandable given the incomprehensible mystery of the union of the infinite (God) and the finite (man) in one person. In writing this book, then, I am conscious that if more work is needed in helping us to be good 'Christologists' it falls especially in the area of knowing the person of Christ. After all, is it not paramount that we have correct views about the one we believe is 'distinguished among ten thousand' (S. of S. 5:10)?

The structure of this book is simple. First, I will provide an understanding of who Jesus is (that is his person). Second, I will look briefly at Christ's work as prophet, priest, and king in his twofold state of humiliation and exaltation. Readers must keep in mind that my main focus in this book is helping Christians to come to a better understanding of the person of Christ, so that even the section on his work will highlight the organic connection between what he did and who he is. Finally, we will look at the glory of Christ. The goal of redemption is the believer's vision of that glory. This vision constitutes true blessedness (or the 'beatific vision'). The vision and glory of Christ in that vision have an organic connection to doctrines about his person and work, and represent the culmination of all Christology. For as the study of doctrines about Christ results (ideally) in an apprehension of him by faith, so faith results, inevitably, in our one day beholding the glory of God in the face of his beloved Son (2 Cor. 3:18).

I am very thankful to Philip Ross who first contacted me and encouraged me to write this book. He reminded me of my 'fearfully expensive' book on Thomas Goodwin's Christology. This book is not a summary of my work on Goodwin, but I acknowledge a great deal of intellectual debt to Goodwin and to John Owen, whose writings on Christ remain, for me, the model for Christian theologians: rigorous interaction with the text of Scripture; a comprehensive understanding of the broader Christian tradition; and an incessant desire to make sure that the profound truths of Christ the mediator are applied to the hearts and minds of those he mediated for.

This is not technically an academic book, but a book for everyone, so I have sought to keep it simple, which is not always easy given the topic under consideration. There are a host of other areas of Christology that have not been discussed (for example, the names of Christ) that are worthy of a book-length project. The specific areas I have chosen are deliberate given what I believe to be a dearth in popular works on Christology.

The feedback provided by Ruben and Heidi Zartman has been invaluable; their labors in reading through this manuscript have contributed to the merit of this book. My doctoral student, Rev. Ryan McGraw, also provided numerous suggestions that I have been happy to take on. I would also like to thank my congregation at Faith Vancouver Presbyterian Church for their constant encouragement and their desire to hear Christ preached weekly from the pulpit. As always, I thank my wife, who has acted as a superwoman over the last year with the arrival of our twin boys, Thomas and Matthew.

I take this opportunity to dedicate this book to two older couples in my congregation who have been particularly helpful to (and patient with) their young minister: Don and Chris Robertson, and Paul and Bernace Walker.

THE CHALCEDONIAN CREED

The finest ecumenical statement on the person of Christ comes from the well-known fifth century document, the Chalcedonian Creed (451 AD). After many intense and complicated debates, the council of bishops present at Chalcedon agreed on the following statement:

We, then, following the holy Fathers,
   all with one consent,
     teach men to confess one and the same Son,
     our Lord Jesus Christ,
     the same perfect in Godhead
       and also perfect in manhood;
truly God and truly man,
   of a reasonable soul and body;
consubstantial with us according to the manhood;
in all things like unto us, without sin;
begotten before all ages of the Father
     according to the Godhead,
   and in these latter days,
   for us and for our salvation,
   born of the virgin Mary,
   the mother of God,
     according to the manhood;
one and the same Christ,
     Son,
     Lord,

Only-begotten,
to be acknowledged in two natures,
inconfusedly,
unchangeably,
indivisibly,
inseparably;
the distinction of natures
being by no means taken away by the union,
but rather the property of each nature being preserved,
and concurring in one Person and one Subsistence,
not parted or divided into two persons,
but one and the same Son,
and only begotten,
God the Word,
the Lord Jesus Christ,
as the prophets from the beginning
have declared concerning him,
and the Lord Jesus Christ himself taught us,
and the Creed of the holy Fathers
has handed down to us.

This ecumenical creed has been embraced by the Western church. The issue before us is how we relate the biblical evidence about Jesus of Nazareth with the Chalcedonian affirmation of one person who has two natures. This is not easy, but it is glorious; and when speaking about the Lord of glory (1 Cor. 2:8) we should expect nothing less, despite our own frailties in knowledge of divine truths.

1

THE PERSON OF CHRIST

Questions are often a valuable way to understand truth. A number of questions could be asked in order to help us understand the person of Christ. For example, when Jesus was a young man helping his father Joseph in carpentry, would it have been appropriate for Jesus to ask what a certain tool was? Or, because he was also fully God, did Christ already know the answer, thus making any question superfluous? Again, we could ask, did Christ, who is the eternal Son of God, need to pray? Or did he merely pray as an example for believers? A trickier question—one that most answer wrongly, in my experience—is: does Christ have one will or two wills? Moreover, did he live by faith or by sight while he ministered on earth? And did he retain his human nature after going to heaven? These questions and many more have been answered in different ways by thoughtful Christians. Our answers to these questions depend entirely upon the view we have of Christ's person.

Perhaps we should consider a more fundamental question before we answer the others, that is: Why did Christ come to earth? Christology involves understanding the person and work of Christ—his person ordinarily discussed in Scripture before his work (see John 1 and Heb. 1–2). These two aspects of Christology are so inter-related that it is practically impossible to discuss his person without also discussing his work. Nor is it possible to appreciate his work apart from understanding who he is; and knowing who he is enables us to understand why he alone is able to save sinners!

CUR DEUS HOMO?
('WHY DID GOD BECOME MAN?')

As a starting point for the investigation of Christology, I will consider the question posed by the brilliant eleventh-century theologian, Anselm of Canterbury (1033–1109). He wrote a famous work titled *Cur Deus homo?*, which may be translated 'Why did God become man?' This question has been answered differently by many great theologians, even those from within the same theological tradition.

One can detect obvious strains of Anselm's thinking in Reformed theologians during the time of the Reformation and indeed in subsequent centuries. For example, following Anselm's thought on the necessity of Christ's satisfaction, theologians such as John Calvin and John Owen held to the view that Christ came into the world to repair the damage done by sin.[1] However, the Puritan theologian Thomas Goodwin argued that Christ was ordained as mediator for 'higher ends' than the salvation of God's people. According to Goodwin, the principal reason that the Son of God became man was not that sinners might be saved by his meritorious work, though of course that was also a reason. Rather, in Goodwin's view, the benefits procured by Christ 'are all far inferior to the gift of his person unto us, and much more the glory of his person itself. His person is of infinite more worth than they all can be of.'[2] Therefore, God's 'chief end was not to bring Christ into the world for us, but us for Christ…and God contrived all things that do fall out, and even redemption itself, for the setting forth of Christ's glory, more than our salvation.'[3] These are remarkable words. But Goodwin was not alone in his view. Another Puritan, Stephen Charnock, equally affirmed that there is 'something in Christ more excellent and comely than the office of a Saviour; the greatness of his person is more excellent, than the salvation procured by his death.'[4] Perhaps the most glorious statement on Christ's person comes from Paul's letter to the Colossians where he speaks of Christ as the 'image of the invisible God' (Col. 1:15; see also Heb. 1:3). The words that follow from that proclamation of Christ's person indicate that all that Christ has done, and continues to do, depend on and reflect the glory of his person.

I cannot help but think that the emphases of Goodwin and Charnock are sorely missing in many modern treatments on the topic of Christology—and perhaps even in our own views of Christ—where the glory of his person takes an obvious back-seat to what he has done for us. The glory of Christ is not an appendix to the topic of Christology. As it is the culmination of all we can say about his person and work, so his glory provides the most basic reason for saying it, in that it is the basis for and the fullness of our eternal enjoyment of him in Heaven. So to answer Anselm's question, we are surely not incorrect to emphasize the need for salvation as one end for Christ's incarnation; but we are not speaking the whole truth if we make Christ's personal glory subservient to our salvation. As the prophet Isaiah wrote, God speaks of his children as those who are 'called by [his] name, whom [he] created for [his] glory, whom [he] formed and made' (Isa. 43:7).

CHRISTOLOGY 'FROM ABOVE'

In discussing the incarnation of the Son of God we have no choice but to begin our Christology from 'above' rather than from 'below'. Starting from 'above' is reflective of the pattern one finds in the New Testament that focuses first on the divinity ('above') of Christ and then on his humanity ('below'). One only has to look at the prologue in John's Gospel where the first verse speaks unambiguously about Christ's divine nature and personhood. John then moves to verse 14 where he affirms that the Word who is 'face-to-face' with God, and is God, has 'become flesh'. If Romans 3:21ff represents Paul's nuclear bomb against Pharisaic religion, then surely John could have said nothing more contrary to Jewish conceptions of Jesus than that the Word, who is Yahweh, became flesh.

The author of Hebrews also begins with a Christology from 'above'. Comparing Hebrews 1 and 2 shows that chapter 1 gives fuller treatment to the divinity of Christ whereas chapter 2 focuses principally on his humanity. A final example, from among many texts that could have been chosen, is Paul's 'Christ-hymn' in Philippians 2, a most significant statement for informing our view of Christ. One detects a high-low-high movement where the eternal divine Son becomes a servant by humbling himself through the incarnation and the obedience of the crucifixion. Yet the God-man is exalted by the Father because of his obedience to death on a cross and he is given the divine name, 'Lord'. More will be said later on this section in Philippians, but clearly the Christology in this hymn begins from 'above' and not from 'below'. This point is absolutely vital if we are going to appreciate the person of Christ.

Why is this important? There is a tendency in our minds to think of Christ as a 'superman'. That is, we fail to believe adequately that he is 'very God of very God' (*autotheos*—God of himself), equal in every way with the Father and the Holy Spirit. Viewing Christ as a sort of 'superman' also prevents us from appreciating his true humanity. Of course, like the doctrine of the

Trinity, the fact of the incarnation is a great mystery and its full truth lies beyond our finite comprehension. That many Christians have managed this mystery by thinking of Christ as a 'superman' explains why certain heresies (for example Arianism and the Jehovah's Witnesses) have flourished and still flourish at precisely these points of theology. A default mode of many theological errors begins when we try to manage God in our own thinking, rather than being content with the many mysteries of the Christian religion that go beyond our reason.

Arianism refers to the fourth century 'archetypal Christian heresy' that denied the divinity of Christ. Arius of Alexandria (c. 250–336) promulgated the view that the Logos was the Son and Servant of God, but not co-equal with God the Father. Arius viewed the Son as a power of God and thus a creature. Hence the famous Arian dictum that there was a time before the Son of God or there was a time when the Son of God was not. In the Post-Reformation period the Socinians held to basically an Arian view of the Son; and today a number of cults, including the Jehovah's Witnesses, also hold to an Arian view.

THE DIVINE SON

A number of fine treatments proving the divinity of Jesus can be found throughout the centuries. As noted, our Christology must begin from above because that is the general picture one finds in the New Testament. In addition to John 1 and Hebrews 1, what other evidences are there that Jesus has a divine nature that is equal with that of the Father and the Holy Spirit? The way in which John in the book of Revelation uses the book of Isaiah provides indisputable proof that Jesus is the divine Son of God.

Consider the following passages:

YHWH (Isaiah)	Jesus (Revelation)
41:4 I, the Lord, the first, and with the last; I am he.	1:17 Fear not, I am the first and the last, and the living one.
44:6 I am the first and I am the last; besides me there is no god.	2:8 And to the angel of the church in Smyrna write: 'The words of the first and the last, who died and came to life.'
48:12 I am he; I am the first, and I am the last.	22:13 I am the Alpha and the Omega, the first and the last, the beginning and the end.

There is no question that John, whose knowledge of the Old Testament is remarkable, believed without any doubt that the resurrected Lord of glory is not only human, but also the divine Lord. John ascribed the divine name to Jesus. Exodus 3:14 explains what the divine name (YHWH) means. As translated in the ESV it means 'I AM WHO I AM.' From the context we could also well translate YHWH as either 'I will be who I will be' or 'I will be who I have been', a rendering that speaks of God's eternity and immutability. This means that the language of Isaiah about the first and the last would be a restating of the divine name, and John's claim that Jesus is the Alpha and Omega (Rev. 22:13) means that Jesus is YHWH.

John makes another reference to Isaiah which proves the divinity of Christ. In Isaiah 6 the prophet sees a vision of 'the King, the LORD of hosts' (Isa. 6:5). No one disputes that Isaiah was given a vision of God. But John, quoting a large section of Isaiah 6, asserts in his gospel that Isaiah 'said these things because he saw [Jesus'] glory and spoke of him' (12:41). Moreover, because Jesus is the LORD (Yahweh), he can petition his Father to glorify him in his Father's presence 'with the glory that [he] had with [his Father] before the world existed' (John 17:5). Of course, in Isaiah we read that God gives his glory to no one else (Isa. 42:8), which means that Christ is either making an abominable request to which he has no rightful claim, or he is in fact entitled to the divine glory that belongs to him as the eternal Son of God.

Paul also makes use of the language in Isaiah in the Christ-hymn (Phil. 2:5–11) to prove Christ's divinity. Verse 6 ('who, though he was in the form of God') may appear to be the obvious place where Paul establishes that the humbled servant is also the eternal God, but verses 9–11 have an important background in Isaiah 45:22–3.

In Philippians 2:9–11 Paul affirms that God has granted to Jesus the glory that, according to Isaiah, belongs to God alone. In Isaiah 45:22–3 'every knee shall bow' to God. Paul is saying therefore that Jesus enjoys the same status as Yahweh. This makes perfect sense in light of the earlier part of the Christ-hymn (v. 6 'who, though he was in the form of God, did not count equality with God a thing to be grasped'), and shows above all that the 'name' (v. 10) in question is the Tetragrammaton (YHWH). Thus Jesus is not merely a lord, but the divine Lord. Note the connection:

Isaiah 45:22–23	Philippians 2:9–11
Turn to me and be saved, all the ends of the earth! For I am God, and there is no other. By myself I have sworn; from my mouth has gone out in righteousness a word that shall not return: 'To me every knee shall bow, every tongue shall swear allegiance.'	Therefore God has highly exalted him and bestowed on him the name that is above every name, so that at the name of Jesus every knee should bow, in heaven and on earth, and under the earth, and every tongue confess that Jesus Christ is Lord, to the glory of God the Father.

THE INCARNATION: GOD'S GREATEST WONDER

Among the many mysteries in the Christian religion, the incarnation is, with the trinity, the most wondrous. Some scholars have assumed that the Eastern Orthodox tradition has done more justice to the centrality of the incarnation than the Western tradition, where one finds an emphasis on the atonement (and sometimes the resurrection). This is more of a caricature than truth. Reformed theologians cherished the incarnation. They wrote often of the incarnation as the greatest wonder that God ever did. To borrow a phrase from Thomas Goodwin, heaven kissed earth when God became man. Do we realize how wonderful this truth is?

In this union between two natures there is the greatest distance involved. The Creator is identified with a creature. In the union of the two natures one sees eternity and temporality, eternal blessedness and temporal sorrow, almightiness and weakness, omniscience and ignorance, unchangeableness and changeableness, infinity and finitude. All of these disparate attributes come together in the person of Jesus Christ. In order to not make God into a man or man into God, we must be careful to insist that the eternal Son of God assumed a human *nature*, not a human *person*. Christ was a man; he had a real human nature, which included a reasonable soul. But he was never a person considered apart from the Son of God. The human nature of Christ subsists in the personhood of the Son of God. If Christ's human nature had a distinct personality, then there would have been two persons united together. But this is clearly unacceptable.

The technical term for the Logos's assumption of a human nature (as opposed to the assumption of another person) by the Logos is 'anhypostasis'. This speaks to

Nestorianism is the view that there are two separate persons in Christ—a human person and a divine person. Many ascribe this view to Nestorius of Constantinople (c. 381–452), but this would be grossly unfair to his teaching, which was basically orthodox. 'Nestorianism' is wrong because the Son assumed a true human nature (body and soul) but not a distinct human person, who already possessed an identity. Hypothetically, if the Son had assumed a distinct individual, then only that individual—and nobody else—could have been saved by the Son.

the human nature being 'personalized' ('hypostatized') by the Logos. Hence the statement that 'the Word became flesh' (John 1:14) is a statement of this personal union of two natures, not a statement that the divine nature somehow changed into a human one. The divine essence is incapable of alteration and communication. Theologians refer to this union as the hypostatic union— the union between the divine and human natures in the person of Christ. Because of the hypostatic union, we speak of Christ as a 'complex person'; that is, unlike the person of the Father or of the Holy Spirit, the person of Christ since the incarnation always involves two natures (though again, manifestly not two persons).

This may be hard to grasp. I think this may be in part because what I am arguing is that the hypostatic union of two natures in one person does not require a single psychological center, as if the 'mind' of the Son of God assumed a human body only. We may be used to making the personal synonymous with the psychological. By 'person' I mean the identity of Christ, who is 'to be acknowledged in two natures, inconfusedly, unchangeably, indivisibly, [and] inseparably' (Chalcedonian Creed). Whatever is natural to the human nature, apart from sin, must be affirmed of Christ, just as whatever belongs to the divine nature must likewise be affirmed of him. This is the wonder of the incarnation. So by assuming a human nature he assumed a human body and soul with a distinct psychology that must not be equated with God's own self-consciousness. More must be said, however, of the nature of Christ's humanity.

> Apollinarianism derives from its founder, Apollinaris of Laodicea (c. 315–392) who fiercely opposed the Arians of the fourth century. But in doing so, he made a fatal error, namely, that in the incarnation the Son did not assume a human mind. Instead, a divine 'mind' (soul) assumed a human body. This error is very common in today's church. The Son united himself to a true human nature, which included a 'reasonable soul and body' (so Chalcedon). The modalist heresy treats the one being of God as absolute and the three persons as derivative so that the Father, the Son, and the Holy Spirit do not reflect who God is in himself. The church's confession of God as three eternally distinct persons in indivisible union is the biblical foundation for a proper understanding of the individual and the corporate in Scripture.

Following the basic thought of Anselm, the Son had to assume a human nature in order to save the bodies and souls of his people. But did Christ assume a human nature in its perfection? This has been a particularly knotty question for theologians from almost all traditions. The Scriptures point to the idea that the human nature of Christ was sinless, but that it suffered from the infirmities that were a part of the curse of man's fall into sin. The words of John 1:14—'the Word became flesh'—seem to suggest that Christ took a human nature that was clothed with infirmities as a consequence of the Fall. Note also Paul's language in Romans 8:3, 'By sending his own Son in the likeness of sinful flesh'. In discussing what is meant by 'flesh' or the 'likeness of sinful flesh' we must tread with some caution.

Christ clearly did not take on all of the infirmities that characterized man's nature after the Fall. The distinction must be made between 'painful infirmities' and 'sinful infirmities'. Of the latter sort, Christ was entirely free. Regarding the former, however, it seems Christ only partook of one aspect of the 'painful infirmities'. That is to say, the 'painful infirmities' of human beings may be divided into those which manifest themselves in the form of disease (for example, leprosy) and those which are 'natural', such as pain, grief, and sorrow. As far as we know, Christ was not subject to disease, such as leprosy. Yet the Scriptures plainly affirm that he was 'a man of sorrows, and acquainted with grief' (Isa. 53:3). In sum, regarding painful infirmities, while we never read that Christ experienced any form of disease or unwellness, it is affirmed that he experienced grief and pain. That is to say, Christ is similar to us in all things, since we are humans, but not according to all of the weaknesses of our nature. Below we will aim to show, given this model, how we may speak of Christ's truly human experiences. Before we do that a common misconception must be removed from how we think of the incarnation.

Some Christians in the pew, and even some theologians, have maintained that Christ's divine nature took the place of his soul. While they are prepared to affirm that Christ had a human body, they think that Christ's soul was somehow the person of the Son of God. But because Jesus was fully human, he had a soul which was the immediate principle of his moral acts, just as our soul is. If he did not have both a human body and a human soul, then the incarnation did not entirely take place, and some aspect of our humanity could not be redeemed. As the Early Church Father, Gregory

Nazianzen famously declared: 'For that which He has not assumed He has not healed.'[5]

In summary, Stephen Charnock depicted the wonder of this well: 'What a wonder is it, that two natures infinitely distant, should be more intimately united than anything in the world; and yet without any confusion! That the same person should have both a glory and a grief; an infinite joy in the Deity, and an inexpressible sorrow in the humanity! That a God upon a throne should be an infant in a cradle; the thundering Creator be a weeping babe and a suffering man, are such expressions of mighty power, as well as condescending love, that they astonish men upon earth, and angels in heaven.'[6] The incarnation is indeed God's greatest work.

Could God himself have performed a greater work than the incarnation?

TWO NATURES AND ONE PERSON: SO WHAT?

All Christians are bound to affirm the truth of the incarnation, the fact that God became flesh. However, the most glorious truths are always the most disputed truths. Often fierce theological debates precede the writing of Creeds. This was certainly true of the ecumenical Creeds, such as the Nicene Creed (325 AD) and the Chalcedonian Creed (451 AD). The Chalcedonian Creed makes statements about the person of Jesus Christ that all Christians must affirm if they wish to call themselves orthodox. Nonetheless, not all Christians have interpreted this Creed in the same way. Some argue that its brevity allows for some diversity. That various traditions interpreted Chalcedon differently is without question, and the key to understanding this diversity is to see it as a result of an intense Christological conflict in the fifth century between the Alexandrian and Antiochene schools of thought. These schools are historically tied to their representative theologians, Cyril of Alexandria (Alexandria) and Nestorius (Antioch).[7] Given the brevity of this book, there is not enough space to look at their various arguments. Nonetheless, the Chalcedonian Creed seems to be a document that both traditions could affirm, one that (perhaps to the surprise of some) Nestorius was relatively happy with.

Scholars continue to debate which side came out victorious in terms of the Creed's language. Nevertheless, most admit that the Creed contains the Alexandrian emphasis on the unity of the person and his divinity, and the Antiochene emphasis on the distinction between the two natures. Perhaps an overly-simplistic response to this would be to suggest that both emphases are entirely consistent with one another. After all, do we not confess that Jesus of Nazareth is one person with two natures? Of course. But the major point of contention in the debate concerned the identity of the person. In other words, do we simply identify the person with the Logos (the Alexandrian position) or with the whole Christ (the Antiochene position—and also John Calvin's)? That question, which will be answered below, has particular significance for how we arrive at a distinctly Reformed Christology.

In the Western Church, theologians have insisted on a distinction between the two natures of Christ, who is *homoousios* ('of one substance/essence') with humanity and *homoousios* with God. However, Roman Catholic, Lutheran and Reformed theologians all understood this distinction differently. Typically, Roman Catholic theologians—though even in this tradition there are a number of various trajectories on most points of theology—understood the union of the two natures (the hypostatic union) in a way that meant that the divine nature, to use Herman Bavinck's words, 'completely permeates and sets aglow the human nature, as heat does iron, and makes it participatory in the divine glory, wisdom and power.'[8] Divine gifts, not divine attributes, are immediately communicated to the human nature of Christ at the incarnation. Because of this, Christ was not only a pilgrim on earth, but one who fully understood all that was possible for the human nature to understand. Unlike believers, who walk by faith, and not by sight, Christ walked by sight.

Bavinck adds that according to this view Christ therefore did not live by faith or in hope because 'all the gifts of which the human nature of Christ was capable were given him, not gradually but all at once, at his incarnation [...] His increase in wisdom (Luke 2:52) must be understood not objectively but subjectively. It seemed so to others; also, when he prayed he did not pray out of need, but only for our sake, to give us an example. Actually Jesus was never a child; he was a man from the start.'⁹ From a Roman Catholic perspective, then, some of the questions addressed above have been answered because of how they speak of the relation between the two natures of Christ. Jesus did not need to ask his father what a certain tool was useful for since he already knew; and he did not need to pray because he lived by sight, not by faith.

Roman Catholic Christology finds a counterpart in Lutheranism. Again, while it is likewise not a monolithic tradition, Lutheran Christology can be basically summarized as the idea that in the hypostatic union the divine attributes are communicated to Christ's human nature. The Lutherans still maintained a distinction between the two natures of Christ, but they claimed that many of the divine attributes are immediately and directly possessed by the human nature at the incarnation. So, for example, omnipotence is communicated to Christ's human nature. Reformed theologians found this not only unacceptable, but nonsensical.

Omnipotence belongs to the essence of God. In other words, to be omnipotent is to be God. And God's essence cannot be divided. Theologians call this the 'simplicity of God', that is, he is not made up of different parts; and so his wisdom is his power, his power is his goodness, and so forth. Since God's essence cannot be divided, if omnipotence were communicated to Christ's human nature so would be every other attribute, including eternity and self-existence. The human nature would have become God, even though God cannot change or become anything. This would mean, of course, that Christ simply had no human nature.

A further implication is that Christ did not receive his humanity in time because eternity would be communicated to the human nature. This explains how Christology was so intimately connected to the Lord's Supper debates: the Lutherans insisted on the bodily presence of Christ in the Lord's Supper and so they had to speak of the ubiquity of Christ's human nature, which was a unique way of understanding the relation of attributes in the person of Christ. Bavinck is certainly correct to argue that both Roman Catholic and Lutheran theologians 'agree in the sense that both elevate the human nature above the boundaries set for it and dissolve into mere appearance both the human development of Jesus and the state of his humiliation.'[10]

Reformed theologians rejected both views on the relation of the two natures. They did this because of an important logical and theological maxim, namely that the finite is not capable of the infinite, or the finite cannot

Eutychianism refers to the views of Eutyches of Constantinople (378–454) who was vague about understanding the relation between Christ's two natures. In short, his error stemmed from 'mixing' Christ's humanity and divinity, which means that his view of Christ will not allow for Christ having a humanity 'like ours in every way' (Heb. 2:17). Note also the words of the Chalcedonian Creed, 'to be acknowledged in two natures, inconfusedly, unchangeably,' which counter the Eutychian view. Theologians from various traditions have (perhaps unfairly) criticized Lutheran Christology for being Eutychian in some respects.

comprehend the infinite. This maxim was not only true of Christ's two natures in his state of humiliation, but even in his state of exaltation. This meant, therefore, that Christ's human nature had limitations; it meant that Christ actually developed from infancy into manhood. It also meant that there was an actual—not pretended—movement from humiliation to exaltation at his resurrection. This is why Christ could say at one point in his ministry: 'But concerning that day and hour no one knows, not even the angels of heaven, nor the Son, but the Father only' (Matt. 24:36; cf. Luke 2:52). This text speaks of the kind of limitation and development which was only possible if Christ's two natures are distinct and real.

The above shows that insisting on the distinction between the two natures in the one person is not enough. The more fundamental question for us concerns how the two natures relate to one another in the person of Christ. This is where Reformed theology is at its very best.

2

THE GREATEST MAN WHO EVER LIVED

THE 'COMMUNICATION OF PROPERTIES'

How Christ's two natures relate to each other is a hugely important theological question. As noted above, it is one thing to affirm that Christ is one person who has two natures, but it is entirely another thing to give a coherent account of how Christ's two natures relate to each other. Reformed theologians typically made use of the phrase, 'the communication of properties', to explain this relation. In the *Westminster Confession of Faith* the so-called 'communication of properties' is explained in language that is relatively simple to understand: 'Christ, in the work of mediation, acts according to both natures, by each nature doing that which is proper to itself; yet, by reason of the unity of the person, that which is proper to one nature is sometimes in Scripture attributed to the person denominated by the other nature' (8.7). These words are exceedingly important. What the Confession affirms here is the view that Christ, the God-man, acts according to both natures. What does this mean?

Christ's authoritative works (for example forgiving sins, substitutionary death) are possible because of his divine nature. Yet his works of ministry were from his manhood. However, because both natures are united in one person, his works are the works of the God-man, not simply the works of a man. This aspect of Christology proved to be a major source of disagreement between Reformed and Roman Catholic theologians. Roman Catholic theologians, like Robert Bellarmine, affirmed that Christ was mediator according to his human nature only, for otherwise if Christ is truly God then God is mediating with himself. Reformed theologians maintained that Christ must be understood as he is God, as he is man, and as he is the God-man (mediator). As God, he is equal with the Father and the Spirit. As man, he is—and always will be—subordinate to the Father and the Spirit. In his mediatorial office, the Son voluntarily subordinates himself to the Father and mediates on behalf of the elect. The works that Christ did, then, were not simply the works of a human; they are the works of the mediator, who is both fully God and fully man. Therefore the value of Christ's death is infinite because of the worth of the person. In other words, one who was a human being only could not have paid the debt owed to God for so great a number of people. Yet because Christ had a true human nature he was able to pay the debt on behalf of sinful humanity.

In the Scriptures there are several examples where the Reformed version of the communication of properties enables us to make sense of the text. The most cited example comes from Acts 20:28 where we read, 'Pay careful attention to yourselves and to all the flock, in which the Holy Spirit has made you overseers, to care for the church of God, which he obtained with his own blood.' Although scholars dispute how to translate this verse, I am persuaded the ESV is correct to convey the impression that the church was purchased by the blood of God. Of course God does not have blood, but Christ, being a true human being, could shed his blood on the cross. Based on the doctrine of the communication of attributes 'that which is proper to one nature is sometimes in Scripture attributed to the person denominated by the other nature' (*WCF* 8.7). Thus the human blood shed on the cross can be called the blood of God because it was the blood of Christ who is God. This shows also how important it is to maintain the unity of Christ's person. Another example is Christ's famous declaration in John 8:58: 'Jesus said to them, "Truly, truly, I say to you, before Abraham was, I am."' The force of this statement was not lost to the Jews who responded by picking up stones to throw at him because, in their minds, this was blasphemy. Christ was born roughly thirty years before he said these words, but because he is not simply a man but also fully God (the eternal Son), he can make a statement in the flesh about his eternal self-existence.

In connection with this doctrine, Reformed theologians have carefully distinguished between the whole Christ and the whole of Christ. The whole Christ is omnipresent, but not the whole of Christ. The unity of the person allows for the former, but the distinction of the two natures means the whole of Christ cannot be omnipresent. In other words, the whole Christ relates to his person, who is of course omnipresent according to his divinity, but the whole of Christ speaks of his two natures, and the human nature is not omnipresent.

DOES CHRIST HAVE ONE OR TWO WILLS?

The above has made plain that Christ is both fully God and fully man; he has two natures, but he is one person. Often I ask various people, from candidates at Presbytery to members in my congregation, does Christ have one or two wills? More often than not, though not exclusively, most people answer the former—Christ has one will. But this is incorrect. The Early Church wrestled with this question, with the monothelites (those who affirmed that Christ had only one will) being condemned in 680–681 when the Sixth Ecumenical Council (Council of Constantinople III) rejected monothelitism and affirmed duotheletism (he had two wills). Some take the union of the two natures in one person to mean that this implies one will. The problem with this type of thinking is essentially the same problem that Lutherans encounter when they speak of the communication of divine attributes to the human nature of Christ. The will of God is an essential attribute, and so to communicate that particular attribute is to communicate all of God's attributes—an ontological impossibility.

Moreover, Christ would not be properly human if his will was divine. As a true human being he necessarily had a true human will. But because he is fully God he has a divine will as well. Thus Christ has two wills. The importance of this cannot be overstated. Christ's human will was necessary for him to render true obedience in

Therefore we declare that in him there are two natural wills and two natural operations, proceeding commonly and without division: but we cast out of the Church and rightly subject to anathema all superfluous novelties as well as their inventors: to wit, Theodore of Pharan, Sergius and Paul, Pyrrhus, and Peter (who were archbishops of Constantinople), moreover Cyrus, who bore the priesthood of Alexandria, and with them Honorius, who was the ruler of Rome, as he followed them in these things. Besides these, with the best of cause we anathematize and depose Macarius, who was bishop of Antioch, and his disciple Stephen (or rather we should say master), who tried to defend the impiety of their predecessors, and in short stirred up the whole world, and by their pestilential letters and by their fraudulent institutions devastated multitudes in every direction. Likewise also that old man Polychronius, with an infantile intelligence, who promised he would raise the dead and who when they did not rise, was laughed at; and all who have taught, or do teach, or shall presume to teach one will and one operation in the incarnate Christ ...

The Sixth Ecumenical Council reports to the Emperor on its condemnation of monothelites, including Honorius, Pope of Rome.

the place of his people. People sometimes forget that the doctrine of justification is as much about Christology as it is about soteriology; in fact, Christology is soteriology. The Anabaptists of the sixteenth century held the view that the person of the Logos took a human body only, but that he did not have a complete human nature. Not surprisingly, they rejected the Protestant doctrine of justification by faith alone. This type of thinking must be fiercely resisted for the sake of Christ, whose obedience to the will of his Father was obedience arising out of love for God with his human heart, soul, mind and strength. This obedience was representative obedience so that he was obeying not only for himself, but also for his people, just as Adam's disobedience was representative and transformative for all his posterity (Rom. 5:12–19).

In the Scriptures we notice that the Son is constantly affirming that he is doing the will of his Father. So, in his bread of life discourse, Christ affirms: 'For I have come down from heaven, not to do my own will but the will of him who sent me' (John 6:38). Likewise, in John 10:17–18, Christ claims that the reason his Father loves him is because he laid down his life for the sheep. Then he affirms that his sacrificial death was a charge he received from his Father. Affirming that Christ has one will, not two wills, commits a trinitarian heresy by positing that there are multiple wills in God; for Christ distinguishes his will in these verses from that of the Father. This, also, is unacceptable. God is one in essence and therefore one in knowledge and will. Only the Son was appointed to be incarnate, but this appointment was willed and effected by the three persons because the external works of the Trinity are undivided; that is, all three persons work simultaneously and inseparably in every work of God. Certain works terminate on one person (for example, sanctification is appropriated to the Holy Spirit), even though all three are necessarily involved. To do the will of the Father is to do the will of the triune God. Therefore, Christ's human will was in complete conformity and obedience to the will of God. What the Father required of Christ was complete obedience to his will, even from the time of Jesus' birth. However, before we turn to the nature of Christ's obedience, an important and typically perplexing question needs to be addressed, namely this: Could Christ have sinned?

COULD CHRIST HAVE SINNED?

If we affirm that Christ had two wills, not one, does that leave open the possibility that Christ could have sinned? Or was Christ impeccable? The author of Hebrews explains that Christ was in fact tempted in every way, as we are, but without sin (Heb. 4:15). Does that mean, however, that it was possible for Christ to sin? Some theologians have argued that Christ's temptations were only real if he was able to sin. And there may be some logic to that idea. There is no doubt that according to Christ's divine nature he could not be tempted and so could not sin (James 1:13). But we have also noted how

Christ possessed a real human nature that consisted of body and soul. We also know that Christ was tempted, and these temptations were real.

According to Christ's human nature, to use Donald Macleod's words, 'he felt the appeal of the sinful proposals put to him and he had to struggle with all his might to repel them.'[11] There were, however, no sinful impulses in Christ that originated from within his human nature. Because Jesus had infirmities (see above) he had natural human weaknesses, which, for example, made him subject to hunger. Thus the devil tempted him in that area in the hope that Jesus would not depend on God but upon bread alone. But, returning to our initial question, Was it possible for Christ to give in to the devil's temptations?

The short answer is no. The temptations were certainly real, and all the more so because so much was at stake and Christ could not shrink back even once (Heb. 10:38); but because of the identity of Christ's person, it was impossible for Christ to sin. The American Reformed theologian, W.G.T. Shedd, puts it well: 'When the Logos goes into union with a human nature, so as to constitute a single person with it, he becomes responsible

Docetism derives from the Greek word, *dokesis*, which means to seem/appear. This heresy views Christ's flesh as 'spiritual'. In other words, this early heresy (2nd century) suggests that Christ only seemed to have human flesh and therefore only seemed to suffer and be tempted. On this view, Christ was only a spirit who emitted a fleshly appearance on earth.

for all that this person does through the instrumentality of this nature…Should Jesus Christ sin, incarnate God would sin.'[12] Moreover, an additional consideration is that apart from the question of natural impeccability, it was hypothetically impossible for Christ to sin as it was not in God's decree. Christ's actions are involved in God's sovereign decree in the same way that ours are, with the important difference that Christ is at the center of God's decree whereas we are elected for Christ's glory.

Therefore Christ did not commit any sin during the whole course of his earthly life, though he faced many types of temptations (Heb. 4:15). He persevered sinlessly to the end and for that reason felt the full force of temptations—in a way which we who resist only for a time cannot feel them. The realities of Christ's temptations are heightened because he never gave in to them during his whole life. John Murray addresses this issue with his usual clarity: 'It was his impeccable holiness that added intensity to the grief of temptation. For the holier a person is, the more excruciating is encounter with solicitation of the opposite…In the case of our Lord this is true to an incomparable degree because he was perfect.'[13] Perhaps there is some truth in the idea that in his human nature he was not aware that it was impossible for him to sin—which adds a whole new perspective to the beauty of his holiness. Instead of sinning, Christ lived a life of perfect obedience that began not at his baptism, but from the moment of conception; it was obedience of a degree that we can never fully comprehend in our sinful estate—remember that not only every action, but also every thought he had was directed to its proper end—but obedience that we are nevertheless thankful for and can marvel at.

'YOU MADE ME TRUST YOU
AT MY MOTHER'S BREASTS'

God's plan of salvation is rooted in eternity. Many Reformed theologians from the seventeenth century onwards spoke of salvation in the terms of the eternal covenant of redemption, in which the persons of the Trinity agreed to rescue man from sin. In redemption, the Father purposed, the Son purchased, and the Spirit applied the benefits of Christ's mediatorial work. One sees this trinitarian nature of salvation in Ephesians 1. But if the Son freely concurred in this great work from eternity, it was not the human nature of Christ that concurred in this covenantal agreement. Therefore, there was a renewal of consent at the moment of Christ's incarnation, which was subsequently reaffirmed throughout his life, even to the point of death. Christ's human will consented to the plan of redemption. The words of Hebrews 10:5–7 are instructive:

> Consequently, when Christ came into the world, he said, 'Sacrifices and offerings you have not desired, but a body have you prepared for me; in burnt offerings and sin offerings you have taken no pleasure. Then I said, "Behold, I have come to do your will, O God, as it is written of me in the scroll of the book."'

These words teach us that Christ came to do the will of God. But when did Christ utter these words? This is a hard question and perhaps beyond us to know definitively. However, because there was room for development in Christ's human nature, we can safely argue that he did not utter these words as a new-born baby since he would have needed to learn how to talk like any other child. What we do know is that Jesus 'increased in wisdom and in stature and in favor with God and man' (Luke 2:52). Growing in wisdom and knowledge was something that took place in Christ's own experience and was not, as some have imagined, only how it appeared to others. Rather, according to the third servant song in Isaiah, the Father gave Christ 'the tongue of those who are taught'; in fact, 'morning by morning' the Father woke Christ to be taught. In that same passage we are told that Christ was not 'rebellious' and did not turn 'backward', but gave his 'back to those who strike and [his] cheeks to those who pull out the beard' (Isa. 50:4–6).

When Christ came into the world he trusted his Father at his mother's breasts (Ps. 22:9). No doubt from Jesus' lips God had ordained praise (Ps. 8:2). Thus, to use Thomas Goodwin's language, 'when first he began to put forth any acts of reason…then his will was guided to direct its aim and intentions to God as his Father, from himself as mediator.'[14] As a babe and child Jesus directed his actions, thoughts, and desires to God and his glory. Goodwin adds: 'Thus it was in Christ when an infant, and such holy principles guided him to that, which was that will of God as to him, and to be performed by him;

and which was to sway and direct all his actions and thoughts, that were to be the matter of our salvation and justification, which were to be exerted to the capacity of reason, as it should grow up more and more.'[15]

Based on the third servant song and other related passages from Scripture, we come to the conclusion that Jesus came to a growing understanding of his Messianic calling by reading the Scriptures. He had to learn the Bible just as we must. Of course, he is the greatest theologian who has ever lived. His reading of the Bible would have been free from the problems that beset Christians who wrongly interpret passages and bring their own sinful dispositions to the text. Nevertheless, we must not imagine that Christ had all of the answers as a baby and merely waited to begin his ministry at the age of thirty without putting in hard yet delightful work on a daily basis in obedience to his Father's will. As Christopher Wright notes, the Old Testament enabled Jesus to understand himself. The answer to his self-identity came from his Bible, 'the Hebrew scriptures in which he found a rich tapestry of figures, historical persons, prophetic pictures and symbols of worship. And in this tapestry, where others saw only a fragmented collection of various figures and hopes, Jesus saw his own face. His Hebrew Bible provided the shape of his own identity.'[16] Of course, God's requirements for the kings of Israel were no different for Christ, who would have fulfilled Deuteronomy 17:18–20 in a manner that no other king did.

This helps us appreciate that accomplishing our great

salvation was no easy task for Christ, since he had to study to know what to do. While he was never ignorant of what he needed to know at any stage of his life, he nevertheless was required to learn. And if Christ had to learn about his calling by reading the Scriptures and receiving the daily teaching of his Father, how much more necessary is it for us to apply ourselves diligently to reading Scripture in dependence upon God to learn how we may walk so as to please him?

In John 17:5 Jesus prays, 'Father, glorify me in your own presence with the glory that I had with you before the world existed.' How did he know about the glory that he had with the Father before the world began? (?)

LIVING BY FAITH?

Christians are those who live by faith in the Son of God who loved us and died for us (Gal. 2:20). The life of faith is the way the Christian begins and continues till the day he or she dies and faith then turns to sight. But what about Christ? Did he live by faith? The simple answer is yes; he is the prototype and perfecter of our faith insofar as he is the highest pattern of true faith (Heb. 12:2). Christ was the greatest believer that ever lived. In fact, Christ had a faith for justification; that is, on the basis of one of the many promises he received for being the faithful mediator, he had a faith that God would vindicate him. Christ did not look to another for his righteousness, but he did look to his Father for justification. As the third servant song makes clear, the Lord helped Christ who set his face like a flint and believed that God would not put him to shame, but would instead vindicate him (Isa. 50:8; cf. 1 Tim. 3:16; John 16:8–11).

Christ's faithfulness was exercised not only for himself, but also for his people. The book of Hebrews leaves us in no doubt about this necessary component of what it means to be truly human. Often declarations about Christ's faith are wed together with the promises made to him by the Father. In the same way, believers are likewise commanded to trust God for all of the blessings of salvation promised to the faithful. Hebrews 2 represents one of the clearest testimonies to the humanity of Christ found anywhere in the Bible. In verse 13 of that chapter, Isaiah 8:17 is applied to Jesus who puts his trust in God. As the pioneer of his people's salvation, Jesus becomes the true and faithful believer whose brothers likewise share the same trust and dependence on God. Whatever saving blessings believers receive from Jesus, those blessings must first be true of Christ himself who is the source of eternal salvation (Heb. 5:9). Whether faith (Heb. 2:13), predestination (1 Pet. 1:20), justification (1 Tim. 3:16), sanctification (John 17:19), or glorification

Christ's greatest grace was his faith. His unwavering belief remedied our greatest sin, unbelief. It is theologically correct to say that Jesus had a faith for his justification and sanctification so that we might have a faith for our justification and sanctification.

(John 17:5), these gifts are ultimately given to Christ who then bestows these same gifts upon his bride. The order or plan of salvation is thus Christological, not anthropological: it centers on Christ, not on our experience of salvation. Whatever we receive must come from our Head (i.e., Christ). The reason believers receive faith as the gift of God is Christ's perfect life of faith as he submitted to his Father's will and trusted his Father to sustain and reward him according to the terms of the covenant of redemption.

Hebrews 2 is not, of course, the only word on Christ's faith. Hebrews 5:7–8 provides another graphic picture of what it meant for Christ to be truly human: 'In the days of his flesh, Jesus offered up prayers and supplications, with loud cries and tears, to him who was able to save him from death, and he was heard because of his reverence. Although he was a son, he learned obedience through what he suffered.' Reading these words one cannot help but reject the idea that Christ's prayers were just a show. The full enjoyment of divine love and the life of sight was not Christ's until after his resurrection when he ascended to the right hand of the Father. But before then his distress and anguish were not only external (coming from opposing forces), but also internal whereby he needed to pray to his Father with 'loud cries and tears'.

Just as the gift of faith is rooted in Christ's own faith during his earthly ministry, we might also suggest that believers pray because Christ was the man of prayer. No one ever prayed like Christ. His affections, thoughts, requests, fervency, and reverence were all constituent parts of his prayer life, and there is no question that when he prayed all of heaven remained silent as the Father delighted to hear the cries of his beloved Son. And yet if we conceive of Christ in the way that Lutheran and Roman Catholic theologians have done, it seems to me that we can make no sense of passages like Hebrews 2:13 and 5:7–8. Much more could and should be said regarding Christ's life of faith and prayer (an act of faith), but there is yet one important aspect of Reformed Christology that remains in order to give us a somewhat complete picture of the person of Christ, namely this: in what power did Christ perform miracles, resist temptation, pray to his Father, live by faith, and offer himself up on the cross? The answer may surprise some, but the Scriptures are clear.

CHRIST AND THE HOLY SPIRIT

Suppose we argue that Christ's divine nature acted through the human nature, thus enabling Christ to perform miracles. What room, then, do we leave for the Holy Spirit in the life of Christ? This is an important question, though perhaps one that goes unnoticed by many Christians. In my opinion, the theology of Cyril and the Alexandrian tradition could give no meaningful role to the Holy Spirit in the life of Christ. In fact, I do not think Roman Catholics or Lutherans can give a suitable explanation for how the Holy Spirit relates to Christ in his twofold state of humiliation and exaltation.

Cyril argued that the Logos was the sole effective agent working on the human nature. This asymmetrical relation between the two natures renders the Spirit's work on Christ superfluous. In addition, if the Lutherans are correct that there is a unidirectional communication of attributes (from the divine to the human), then why do the Scriptures give such a meaningful role to the Holy Spirit in relation to Christ's ministry on earth (and in heaven)? As Bavinck noted, 'While Lutheran Christology still speaks of gifts, it actually does not know what to do with them and no longer has room even for Christ's anointing with the Holy Spirit.'[17] Similarly, the Puritan theologian Isaac Ambrose asks, if the Lutheran version of the communication of properties is true, 'to what end should created gifts serve, which Christ hath received above measure?'[18]

Reformed theologians were very careful to insist upon the integrity of the two natures. Thus, as noted above, the finite (human nature) cannot comprehend the infinite (divine nature), not even in the closest possible union, as in the case of Christ. John Owen made a rather remarkable contention in the seventeenth century that might surprise people today. He affirmed that the 'only singular immediate act of the person of the Son on the human nature was the assumption of it into subsistence with himself.'[19] This meant that the Holy Spirit was the 'immediate operator of all divine acts of the Son himself, even on his own human nature. Whatever the Son of God wrought in, by, or upon the human nature, he did it by the Holy Ghost, who is his Spirit.'[20] Owen argues for an unconventional view that has been fiercely resisted by many theologians, probably because some have used similar language in a way that undermines the divinity of Jesus. For most Christians, Jesus performed his miracles because his divine nature operated in and through his human nature. I think this is entirely wrongheaded and fails to account for the explicit Scriptural evidence concerning Christ's earthly ministry.

Sinclair Ferguson correctly observes that the prophet Isaiah viewed the Messiah 'as the Man of the Spirit *par excellence* (Is. 11:1, 42:1; 61:1).'[21] When one considers the major events in Christ's ministry he will note that the Holy Spirit takes a prominent role. Indeed, the term 'Christ', which has become a proper name for Jesus, means 'anointed'. It was by means of that anointing of the Spirit that Christ performed his office of mediator. Thus the Holy Spirit was the immediate (i.e., direct) divine efficiency that enabled the incarnation to take place. The Spirit came upon the virgin Mary and enabled her miraculously to conceive the baby Jesus (Luke 1:31, 35). Incidentally, because of the doctrine of the communication of attributes, it is entirely appropriate to say with Cyril—and Nestorius, by the way—that Mary is the mother of God (*theotokos*). To call Mary the 'mother of God' was never intended by anyone to imply that God had an origin, nor is it about exalting Mary; rather, it is about defending the unity of the person who was conceived and born of Mary according to his human nature. We could likewise speak of James as the 'brother of God'.

The conception of Jesus is a new creation and this act has many parallels with our own new birth; for, if any man is in Christ he too is a new creation (2 Cor. 5:17). The Spirit worked on the humanity of Mary to produce a true human nature that the Son of God took into subsistence with himself, so that the Son is now forever in his identity the God-man. This work of the Holy Spirit was necessary so that the human nature of Jesus could be derived from Mary without any taint of sin, which would have been impossible if the Son had assumed a human nature that was the product of Joseph and Mary. The Spirit not only formed the human nature of the man Jesus, but also remained in him and on him during his childhood where, as we noted above, Jesus would have been reading the Old Testament scriptures and meditating and praying to his Father in heaven (Luke 2:49).

The next major event in Jesus' life was his baptism by John the Baptist in the Jordan. At the beginning of his public ministry Jesus was baptized (and ordained) in a most remarkable manner. Besides the fact that a sinful man baptized the Lord of Glory, we are told that as Christ came out of the water the Holy Spirit descended on him like a dove. In audible voice, the Father addressed Jesus: 'You are my beloved Son; with you I am well pleased' (Mark 1:10). This was not because Jesus had been obedient that day, but also because Jesus had been obedient from his mother's breasts, and for that reason his Father delighted in him. At this point Jesus received the Spirit without measure (John 3:34) and so was publicly constituted Messiah. The Spirit was certainly present with Jesus from the moment of conception, but at his baptism he received the Spirit in even greater measure than before.

Having been baptized, Jesus was driven by the Holy Spirit into the wilderness to be tempted for forty days and forty nights (Mark 1:12). In his holy war against the devil, Christ, in reliance upon the Spirit, quoted Scripture passages that he no doubt learned during his life where the Father woke him 'morning by morning' to be taught (Isa. 50:4). The Spirit who 'drove' Jesus into his temptation sustained Jesus during that temptation. Luke reports that after his temptation 'Jesus returned in the power of the Spirit to Galilee' (Luke 4:14). Luke then reports Jesus' rejection at Nazareth. It is significant that the sermon that led to the attempted murder of Jesus was from Isaiah 61:1–2, a text Jesus used to affirm that the Spirit of the Lord was upon him (Luke 4:18). That is to say, Christ's preaching was always in the power and demonstration of the Spirit. He was the finest preacher who ever lived and the Spirit upon him convicted and converted his hearers to the point that people either

Every blessing we possess is second-hand. They were first all in Christ because Christ was the man of the Spirit *par excellence*. By the enabling of the Spirit, Christ performed his work as Savior and was thus justified, adopted, sanctified, and glorified so that we in turn might also receive those blessings.

hated him or followed him. It was not just the words of Jesus that divided people, but the power of the Spirit accompanying his words left people saying that 'No one ever spoke like this man!' (John 7:46).

Jesus not only preached—though that was the reason why he came (Mark 1:38)—but he also performed many mighty miracles, which were visible evidences that his authority was from God (see Matt. 9:1–8). Christ's performance of miracles is also attributed to the Holy Spirit: 'But if it is by the Spirit of God that I cast out demons, then the kingdom of God has come upon you' (Matt. 12:28; cf. Acts 10:38). Christ performed miracles because the Holy Spirit enabled him. But sometimes Christ could not perform mighty works (Mark 6:5) because the Spirit did not enable him. God's power is greater than man's sin, but nevertheless in Mark 6:5 we have striking testimony to the fact that in his human nature Jesus was entirely dependent upon the Holy Spirit to perform miracles.

The death of Christ is the last major event during his state of humiliation; and it appears that Christ, who in one sense was killed (Acts 2:36), gave up his life freely (John 10:18) in the power of the Holy Spirit. This is confirmed by the language of Hebrews 9:14: 'Christ, who through the eternal Spirit offered himself without blemish to God…'. As Sinclair Ferguson notes, 'A strong case can be made for understanding the *pneuma* in which Jesus offered himself as referring to the divine Spirit.'[22] Jesus committed his human spirit to his Father (Luke 23:46) because the Holy Spirit enabled him to lay down his life. Like his death, Christ's resurrection is attributed to the Spirit (Rom. 8:11) when he is declared 'through the Spirit of holiness…to be the Son of God' (Rom. 1:4). According to the Scriptural evidence, the Holy Spirit was Christ's inseparable companion during his earthly ministry. We must therefore have a Christology that makes sense of the plethora of passages that speak of the Holy Spirit's work on Jesus.

The importance of this cannot be overstated. Christ's obedience in our place needed to be real obedience. He did not 'cheat' by relying on his own divine nature while he acted as the second Adam. Rather, by receiving and depending upon the Holy Spirit, Christ was fully dependent upon his Father (John 6:38). The translation of *ouch harpagmon hegesato* (Phil. 2:6) as 'he did not regard his equality with God as something to exploit' or 'something to take advantage of' fits perfectly with this model. Such an understanding of Christ's life only serves to heighten our appreciation for what he did as the second Adam. Herman Bavinck summarizes the basic theological concerns set forth regarding the intimate relation between the Spirit and Christ: 'The true human who bears God's image is inconceivable even for a moment without the indwelling of the Holy

'We are to know Christ so as to labour after conformity to him; and this conformity consists in a participation of the graces whose fullness dwells in him. And we cannot regularly press after this, but by an acquaintance with the work of the Spirit on his human nature, which therefore deserves our most diligent study' (John Owen).[23]

Spirit…If humans in general cannot have communion with God except by the Holy Spirit, then this applies even more powerfully to Christ's human nature.'[24]

Returning to the relation of the two natures of Christ, we may say that Christ's divine nature did not operate immediately upon his human nature, but mediately by means of the Holy Spirit. The Holy Spirit immediately dwelt on Christ and in Christ. Christ was obedient to his Father at every point; but it was the Spirit who enabled him in that obedience. Thus in Christ's earthly ministry he was subject to the will of the Father and thus to the Holy Spirit. Then in his state of exaltation he became Lord of the Spirit (2 Cor. 3:17). The Spirit even takes on the name of Christ (Rom. 8:9; 1 Pet. 1:11). We will look at this in more detail as we consider Christ's work in his threefold office as the prophet, priest, and king of the church which he purchased with his own blood.

3

THE WORK OF CHRIST

Christology necessarily involves both the person and the work of Christ. The Reformed understanding of Christ's person has significant ramifications for his work, particularly the idea that Christ the mediator moved from a state of humiliation (his earthly ministry) to a state of exaltation (his post-resurrection life). This change was something that Christ himself experienced. We can attribute Christ's movement from humiliation to exaltation to the successful performance of the work the Father had given him to do. As the servant of the Lord who was obedient to death, even death on a cross (Phil. 2:8), Christ experienced a change at the resurrection: he is now the risen, exalted Lord and

Savior of the world who has received promises that were made to him in eternity. Christ not only retains his human nature in heaven—for the hypostatic union of the two natures is an indissoluble union that can never be broken—but he also retains his threefold office as prophet, priest and king until the consummation. So Christ's work is the work of the prophet, priest, and king during his earthly humiliation and heavenly exaltation.

CHRIST AS PROPHET

As prophet, Christ not only foretells and forth-tells the truth, but he is the truth (John 14:6). This is what marks him out as the prophet of God *par excellence*. No man ever spoke like Christ (John 7:46), for Christ spoke with authority (Luke 4:32). As the prophet of the Church of God, Christ reveals to his people, 'by his Word and Spirit, the will of God for our salvation' (*WSC*, 24). The first and fundamental thing that we need to understand about Christ's office of prophet is that he makes theology possible; he is the source of all knowledge. In Christ is the repository of all truth; he is the center of all divine revelation. He makes theology possible because he is not only human but divine. Because in Christ 'are hidden

Jesus Christ had a faith for justification, holiness for sanctification, a name for adoption, and a body for glorification, all in the context of his offices as prophet, priest, and king.

all the treasures of wisdom and knowledge' (Col. 2:3), we must distinguish between the theology that Christ possesses and the theology that we possess. Christ's knowledge and understanding about the mind of God far exceeds that of anyone else who has ever lived or will ever live. We cannot comprehend the mind of God, and likewise we cannot comprehend fully the theology of Christ. In other words, Christ has knowledge of God that is beyond that of all the believers combined, even believers in glory. Because he is the God-man, Christ enables revelation to be communicated from God to humanity. As a prophet, he mediates revelation from God to man in both states, even into eternity.

Christ's great end as a prophet is to declare perfectly the revelation of God (Matt. 13:35; John 1:18). The Scriptures are dependent upon Christ for their content. Typically, Reformed theologians have referred to the theology of pilgrims on earth as 'our theology', which is given by Christ. This revealed theology is finite (ectypal) theology, as opposed to infinite (archetypal) theology, which is the infinite knowledge that God has of himself. This distinction is not only a quantitative distinction, but a qualitative one. Both the content and quality of God's knowledge are infinitely superior to human knowledge.

In the Old Testament the divine Son reveals his will by his divine nature, for he was not yet incarnate. But in the gospel age, after taking on human flesh, he teaches as the prophet sent by God. We may be tempted to think that Christ's ability to reveal the will of God comes from his unique privilege of being one person with two natures, with the eternal Logos enabling Christ to reveal God's will to the church. This is not entirely correct. In his divine nature, Christ is omniscient. But if it were true that Christ's divine nature was the immediate means by which he revealed truth to the church, why then was he ignorant of certain facts during his life (as noted above)? Christ revealed the will of God according to his human nature, not his divine nature. Though the offices are personal, that is, they are carried on by Christ the person, not by an abstracted nature, nonetheless the human nature of Christ is involved in all of his three offices of prophet, priest, and king.

To exercise his office of prophet Christ received the necessary gifts and graces to be able to perform his duty in this office. He had natural, innate abilities, which all men possess. Also, he was free from sin. His mind was, so to speak, firing on all cylinders. But more than that, Christ had, as we have noted above, the peculiar endowment of the Holy Spirit. In addition, while we cannot begin to comprehend what sort of mind this is, we are thankful that he spoke to us the will of God for our salvation. Christ certainly learned from reading the Scriptures, but he was also privileged to receive by means of the Holy Spirit direct communication from God concerning his office as mediator.

Before Christ could reveal new truths to the church that were not yet given in the Scriptures, God had to reveal them to him first. Of course, if God did not reveal certain truths, such as the time of the second coming, then Christ was ignorant of those truths, though only for a short while (see Matt. 24:36; Rev. 1). After his resurrection, Christ's entrance into glory took place via his ascension into heaven where he was seated at the right hand of the Father. At his enthronement Christ received the Holy Spirit in the fullest possible measure that the human nature is capable of. One cannot help but think of the words in Psalm 45:6–7, which are a picture of Christ's enthronement.

> Your throne, O God, is forever and ever. The scepter of your kingdom is a scepter of uprightness; you have loved righteousness and hated wickedness. Therefore God, your God, has anointed you with the oil of gladness beyond your companions.

This relates clearly to Christ's kingly office, but upon closer reflection there is a sense in which Christ's enthronement as the king of kings has important ramifications for his offices of prophet and priest. In terms of his office as prophet, since Christ received the Spirit in such abundant measure, he now possesses in his human nature comprehensive (though not infinite) knowledge of God's decrees and purposes. In other words, Christ always knows what he needs to know. In his glorified humanity his knowledge is as comprehensive as God's decree. Because Christ retains his human nature in heaven, he may in fact still grow in his knowledge in eternity.

Christ's office as mediator will end with the consummation of all things (1 Cor. 15). Nevertheless there is a sense in which he continues to function as prophet of the church in heaven. If what we have said about Christ's prophetic office is true, namely that he is the source of all communications from God to mankind, then what about heaven? John Owen was of the opinion that Christ, in his glorified humanity, will be the mediator of the saints' knowledge and love for the triune God. As Thomas Manton noted, Christ is a 'living Bible' and saints will need no other book when they are in heaven, for they shall read 'much of the glory of God in the face of Jesus Christ.'[25] Owen likewise claims that communications and revelations from God to his redeemed people are through Jesus, 'who shall forever be the medium of communication between God and the church, even in glory. All things being gathered into one head in him, even things in heaven and things in earth...this order shall never be dissolved...and on these communications from God through Christ depend entirely our continuance in a state of blessedness and glory.'[26]

Revelation from the triune God has not ended permanently with the closing of the Canon. That does not mean that God reveals his will for our salvation today as he did during the times of the apostles and the Prophets. An exposition of Ephesians 2:20 and Hebrews 1:1–2 militates against such an idea. Revelation from the triune God in this world has ceased until the consummation; but that does not mean that God has nothing more to reveal. In heaven God will continue to communicate to his saints, and he will do so through Jesus Christ.

CHRIST AS PRIEST

Christ's office of priest has historically been the most debated of all his three offices. Liberal theology has emphasized his office of prophet at the expense of priest and king. But historic Reformed theologians have always recognized the indispensability of all three offices, with a peculiar emphasis on his office as priest. Debates about the nature of the atonement (Christ's death) are debates about Christ's office as priest. But Christ is not only a priest because of his atonement. As the *Westminster Shorter Catechism* makes clear, Christ's priesthood consists of his 'once offering up of himself a sacrifice to satisfy divine justice…and in making continual intercession for us' (A. 25). Christ performs his office as priest in his oblation (sacrificial death) and his intercession. His intercession is a great part of his work as Savior and yet, in my own experience, Christians seem more interested in Christ's death than his intercession. In actual fact, the two are conjoined; his oblation precedes his intercession, and his intercession presupposes his oblation. The application of salvation depends on Christ's intercession. In other words, if Christ does not ascend to heaven and intercede for the saints our salvation is incomplete, and so we are not saved at all. Moreover, Christ's intercession in heaven is a continued oblation of himself insofar as he continually presents its efficacy or completeness in our defense. Christ continually intercedes for us with the Father (Heb. 7:25), who delights in listening to the requests of his Son on our behalf. Christ is not twisting the arm of the Father; but rather in the way God has planned salvation, the Father has ordered that Christ should act as the mediator in order for the Father to shower the church with blessings through his Son and for his Son's sake.

In discussing Christ's office as priest, we are faced yet again with the importance of understanding his person correctly. In order to be a priest Christ must be a man. His humanity meant he was not only able to offer himself up on the cross—a true human substitute in our place—but he is able to sympathize with his people in their weaknesses (Heb. 4:15). On the other hand, his divinity meant he was able to die a meritorious death on the cross that would save not just one sinner, in whose place he stood, but many sinners (see Rom. 5). The worth of Christ's person gave infinite value to his work. In other words, his death was not lacking in sufficiency to save innumerable people because, as we noted above, the person that died on the cross was God (Acts 20:28).

Commonly we think of Christ's office of priest as consisting in his death and intercession. Yet there is also another important aspect of his priesthood that cannot go unnoticed, namely his life of obedience from the manger to the grave. As the second Adam, Christ differed from Old Testament priests insofar as they only offered sacrifices for people, but they did not and could not obey the law for people. The Old Testament priesthood addressed the breach of the law only; but the righteousness that God requires is addressed by the perfectly obedient priest.

The author of Hebrews highlights Christ's ability to be a sympathetic high priest because he himself was tempted since he shared in flesh and blood (Heb. 2:17–18; 4:15). He offered prayers with loud cries and tears (Heb. 5:7), and so the offering up of his life consisted not only in his crucifixion, but also in his voluntary obedience to the law of God. He subjected himself to the curse of God's law by dying a cursed death (Gal. 3:13), but his life as well as his death was an 'oblation' in the sense that it was full of suffering and misery. 'Although he was a son, he learned obedience through what he suffered' (Heb. 5:8); that is, his whole life was a life of suffering, which made him the perfect sacrifice. He learned obedience in the context of being despised and rejected by men (Isa. 53:3). The cross was the consummate act of his obedience (Phil. 2:8), and this was a fitting 'end' for one who had never known a second of disobedience to his heavenly Father. Thus, as a priest, Christ's death was a 'fragrant offering and sacrifice to God' (Eph. 5:2) on account of the beauty of his holiness and the supreme dignity of his person. As an exalted priest Christ has the capacity to sympathize with his people in a manner that goes beyond our comprehension because his sufferings and temptations were of a far greater degree than what we experience.

We need to be aware that Christ was appointed to the office of priest. But he was not an Aaronic priest.

He belonged to the order of Melchizedek (Heb. 5:6, 10), the priest-king spoken of in Genesis 14:18–20 and Psalm 110:4. This order of Melchizedek is eternal and unchangeable, compared to the vanishing Aaronic order. In Hebrews 7:26 we are informed that Christ was a priest who was 'holy, innocent, unstained, separated from sinners, and exalted above the heavens.' Thus he offered himself, not for himself, but for the sins of his people. Almost everything he did was as a 'common person'. As a common person, Christ is a representative of all the people the Father gives to him (John 6:39). In contrast, in his intercession he intercedes not as a common person, but rather on our behalf. In the Old Testament the High Priest entered the holy of holies not for himself, but for the people, which explains why he had the names of the twelve tribes upon his shoulders (Ex. 28:21). Christ's death was therefore a substitutionary death; he died with 'the twelve tribes' (i.e., his elect people) on his shoulders and especially in his heart (S. of S. 8:6). More, his death was a victorious death. By dying he destroyed the devil, who had the power of death, and thus delivered his people from the fear of death (Heb. 2:14–15).

When it comes to understanding Christ's intercessory work it is absolutely vital to have a right view of Christ's person. Jesus informed his disciples that it was for their good that he left them so that the Holy Spirit would

Christ's righteousness, because of the dignity of his person, pleases God more than our sin displeases him.

come to them (John 16:7). This has always been a tricky text to understand, especially if we hold to the (correct) view that the disciples already possessed the Holy Spirit when Christ spoke these words. Christ likely made this statement because the Holy Spirit's ministry to his people on earth reflects his high priestly ministry in heaven.

After ascending into heaven, Christ poured out his Spirit on the church (Acts 2:33; Eph. 4:8). Christ and the Spirit share a oneness of purpose and will. Thus the Spirit persuades believers of Christ's love for them. The Spirit prays in us because Christ prays for us (Rom. 8:26–7); the Spirit is an intercessor on earth because Christ is an intercessor in heaven. Christ no longer lives by faith and hope; all that is left for him now is to live by love alone (1 Cor. 13:13), and Christ's love for his church is enhanced in heaven. As we saw above, upon entering heaven, Christ received the Holy Spirit in the fullest measure that a human being is capable of. Part of the fruit of the Spirit is love; indeed, it is listed first in order, which reflects its priority over other graces. Christ continues to love his people so that he may remain in his Father's love (John 10:15–18; 15:10). The quality of Christ's love and compassion in heaven is better than all men's hearts put together. In fact, as Thomas Goodwin eloquently stated: 'if there were infinite worlds made of creatures loving, they would not have so much love in them as was in the heart of that man Christ Jesus.'[26] The love of God in his divine nature exceeds the love that Christ has in his human nature since the finite does not have the capacity to attain the infinite. Yet Goodwin assures us that there is more than enough love and compassion in Christ's human heart to satisfy his bride. We cannot even begin to fathom how compassionate he is as our High Priest; we can only be assured that he is, and believe that truth according to our measure of faith (Rom. 12:3).

In heaven Christ's execution of his offices is heightened. As prophet he is filled with wisdom and knowledge; as priest he showers grace and mercy upon his church; and as king he is given power and dominion. This means that Christ is more compassionate now in heaven than he was on earth. In other words, if Christ was merciful to sinners during his ministry on earth, he is now more, not less, merciful to sinners. More than that, the incarnation added a new way for God to be merciful. Because God became flesh, an experimental compassion is gained. The divine nature is not capable of temptation. Christ, now in heaven, is able to remember his own condition in the world, one of suffering and temptations. He remembers in heaven the difficulty of his life on earth; he remembers the force of his temptations; and because of this he is able to sympathize with his people in a way that would have been impossible if the incarnation had not happened. It is truly a remarkable thing to suggest that there is a new way for God to be compassionate and

According to his human nature, does Christ love his people even more now in Heaven than when he was on Earth?

merciful, but it is true. Hence one cannot overstate the importance of a proper understanding of Christ's person for appreciating his work, both on earth and in heaven.

CHRIST AS KING

The final office that Christ occupies as the mediator is that of king. In this office he subdues his people to himself by ruling them according to his law, and defending them according to his title as king (i.e., the Son of God). More than that, he conquers all of his and our enemies. Importantly, the Old Testament verse most quoted in the New Testament—22 times, including explicit and implicit references—speaks of Christ sitting at the right hand of the Father where he subdues his enemies (Ps. 110:1).

When we speak of Christ as king we are not speaking about him in his divine nature alone, but, in keeping with the emphases above, we are speaking of the Son as the God-man. Of course, regarding his divine nature, the Son possesses dominion and majesty as an essential attribute. The triune God is King. God's authority is absolute authority and cannot be added to or diminished in any way. But this is not what is in view when we discuss Christ's kingship. Christ is king in reference to his mediatorial role. And because of that, there is a sense in which Christ's kingship undergoes changes, especially in terms of his two states of humiliation and exaltation.

The Psalms provide an important insight into the nature of Christ's kingship. In the first place, one has only to compare Psalm 2 with Psalm 110. These two Psalms share a number of similarities: subjugation of the nations (2:1–3; 110:1–2); destruction of Israel's enemies (2:9; 110:5–6); and God's wrath towards kings who oppose his Son (2:5; 110:5–6). As a Davidic King, Christ is, in a special sense, God's Son. We often assume that Jesus being the Son of God proves his deity, but it is more accurate to hold that first-century Jews would have immediately understood the title 'Son of God' as kingly, as Messianic (see Matt. 16:16). Certainly, Christ is the eternal Son of God, equal with the Father and Spirit in power and glory; but Psalms 2 and 110 have in view earthly kings who are given the unique privilege of being called God's Son. In this sense, the true king, Jesus Christ, shares in his Father's kingship, and yet he is subordinate to his Father's cosmic kingship. Because Christ is God's king (i.e., true Son), victory over his enemies is certain.

In Psalm 110, however, Christ sits at the right hand of the Father. This enthronement is the highest possible authority that can be given to any man (Matt. 28:18). It represents power, honor, and favor. There seem to be some differences between the two Psalms that may reflect the changing nature of Christ's kingship. In Psalm 2:2 the 'rulers take counsel together against the Lord and against his anointed', whereas in Psalm 110:2 Christ rules in the midst of his enemies. In Psalm 2:8 Christ asks for the nations as his inheritance, and in Psalm 110 God uses Christ's rule to fight for his Son. The rulers and nations were summoned to submit to God's

Son (Ps. 2:10–12), but they did not and the wrathful outcome is highlighted in Psalm 110:5–6.

In the New Testament, Psalm 110:1 is used to highlight important truths about Christ's kingship. First, Christ uses this text in his state of humiliation to speak of his transcendence (Mark 12:36). Second, Peter references Psalm 110:1 to speak of Christ's post-resurrection vindication (Acts 2:32–36). Third, in that glorious text, Romans 8:34, Paul connects Christ's kingship with his intercession; this is consistent with Psalm 110, which speaks not only of Christ's kingship, but also of his priesthood (Ps. 110:4). Finally, the New Testament use of Psalm 110:1 clearly speaks of the Lordship of Christ over all creatures, even the angels (Heb. 1:13).

In addition to Psalms 2 and 110, Psalm 8 provides another gateway into understanding Christ's kingship. Psalm 8 is quoted in Hebrews 2:6–8. In my view, Psalm 8 is not explicitly Messianic, at least not in the way that Psalms 22 or 110 are. Hebrews 2:6–8 uses Psalm 8 consistently with Genesis 1:26–28 regarding the created purpose of man (Adam). Hebrews 2:6–8 refers to God's original purpose for mankind. This makes the 'but' at the beginning of Hebrews 2:9 extremely important. Where man, including David (the son of God) has failed (miserably and absolutely), Christ has succeeded vicariously for us all. The rest of the chapter shows that Christ has also acted vicariously for us in his death. Hebrews 2:9 and Psalm 110:1 (cited in Heb. 1:13) show that all things have been placed under Christ's feet. Christ's death and resurrection inaugurate this reality, but the consummation will take place in the future. Thus, the divine commission originally given to Adam is actually fulfilled in Christ who rules the present world and will rule the world to come.

By using Psalm 8:4–6 in Hebrews 2:5–9, the writer gives specific attention to two aspects of Christology: humiliation and exaltation. The Son who is made for a little while lower than the angels, and who said, 'Foxes have holes, and birds of the air have nests, but the Son of Man has nowhere to lay his head' (Luke 9:58), is also the Son of God who is 'crowned with glory and honor' (Heb. 2:9).

Similarly, in 1 Corinthians 15:27 Paul applied Psalm 8 to Christ's reign. Christ's exaltation at God's right hand (see also Rev. 4–5) is the revelation of the true humanity of Christ and the fulfillment of this Psalm. The mandate to subdue and populate the earth in Genesis 1–2 was never realized in Adam. But it was and is being realized in Christ. Hence the great commission (Matt. 28:16–20) is actually the fulfillment of Genesis 1:26ff. Christ has regained authority to subdue the earth and repopulate it with creatures who are true humans. Thus to go and make disciples of all nations fulfills Genesis 1, Psalm 8, and Psalm 110. Though Christ was lower than the angels for a season, he is now supreme in all the universe of men and angels (Heb. 1:1–3), and hence Psalm 8 is implicitly messianic. In celebrating God's unrealized original constitution, Psalm 8 pointed forward to Christ, in whom that purpose is fulfilled. The bigger point in the context of Hebrews 1, of course, is to prove that the incarnate Christ is far superior to the angels. This is true in his divinity (ch. 1), and in his perfect humanity (ch. 2). For Christians, this means that because of our union with Christ we will share in Christ's cosmic victory. We will judge angels (1 Cor. 6); and we will sit with Christ on his throne. Our union with Christ raises us to a place beyond what Adam was promised because we are in solidarity with the God-man. In other words, salvation is not simply what Christ has done for us, but that what is done to Christ will be done to us. In bearing his name, we receive everything that his name deserves (Rev. 3:12).

Because of his obedience to death on a cross, the Father exalts his Son (Phil. 2:9–11). The Son's kingdom is his reward; it is something given to him. He received it not by usurpation, but by the decree and gift of his Father (John 5:22; Acts 2:36; 10:42). For this reason, Christ's kingdom is a temporal (i.e., time-bound) kingdom where the Lord Jesus showers his bride with gifts and defeats his enemies by his resurrected power.

To bestow this kingdom upon Christ, God had to do nine things:

1. Prepare a body for Christ (Heb. 10:5) so that he could be truly human and represent his people.
2. Anoint Christ with the Holy Spirit above measure (John 3:34) to provide him with the requisite endowments for being a godly king (Isa. 11:2).
3. Publicly declare Christ a king (Matt. 3:17; 17:5).

4. Give him a sceptre of righteousness, put a sword in his mouth, and enable him (as a Prophet-King) to reveal the will of God to mankind.
5. Honor Christ with ambassadors and servants (Eph. 4:11–12; 2 Cor. 5:20).
6. Grant to Christ the souls of people, not just Jews but Gentiles also (Ps. 2:8; John 17:6).
7. Give him power to regulate the church according to divine law (Matt. 5; Col. 2:14).
8. Provide him with power to judge and condemn his enemies (John 5:27).
9. Allow Christ to pardon sins (Matt. 9:6). These privileges given to the Son are given to him as the God-man.[28]

When Christ has finally subdued all of his enemies and applied salvation to all his elect people through his Spirit (the Spirit of Christ, Rom. 8:9), he will hand the kingdom over to his Father (1 Cor. 15:24–5). There is some evidence that his mediatorial offices of prophet, priest, and king will come to an end at the consummation. Many sound theologians have likewise affirmed this to be the case. However, I believe that some aspects of Christ's offices will remain into eternity so that he will still be a prophet,

'Our Mediator was called Christ, because he was anointed with the Holy Ghost above measure; and so set apart, and fully furnished with all authority and ability, to execute the offices of prophet, priest, and king of his church, in the estate of both his humiliation and exaltation' (*WLC* 43).

priest, and king. But how? A look at the glory of Christ will help us understand this apparent dilemma.

CHRIST'S THREEFOLD OFFICE HUMILIATED

Christ's threefold office (of prophet, priest, and king) comes under close scrutiny by the gospel writers during his passion. In fact, all three offices are blasphemed. First, his office of prophet is ridiculed: 'Then they spit in his face and struck him. And some slapped him, saying, "Prophesy to us, you Christ! Who is it that struck you?"' (Matt. 26:67–8). He may or may not have known at the time, but he surely does now and at the Day of Judgment he will tell them, unless of course they repented for their heinous actions.

Second, Christ's office as priest is mocked. The words in Matthew 27:42 represent a most remarkable irony: 'He saved others; he cannot save himself.' Little did they know that he was doing precisely that. They unwittingly spoke a glorious truth in their mockery of his saving work as priest. And yet they also lied, for he could have saved himself (John 10:18–19), but instead, for the joy set before him, he endured the cross (Heb. 12:2). How astounding that these mockers may later have been converted and saved by the one they claimed could not save himself (Luke 23:34; Acts 2:36–41).

Third, Christ's kingship is openly questioned and ridiculed: 'He is the King of Israel; let him come down now from the cross, and we will believe in him' (Matt. 27:42). In dying on the cross Christ actually gained the greatest of all victories: the victory over the devil (Heb. 2:14). Never has a king triumphed over his enemies as Christ did on the cross. In heaven now Christ has absolute power over all of his enemies who are his footstool (Ps. 110:1).

THE GLORY OF CHRIST

The glory of Christ should be our chief desire. Hallowing, praising, and thus glorifying the name of Christ is the greatest spiritual calling of the Christian. The most important thing a Christian can do is worship God on the Lord's Day and bring glory to his name. But can we actually 'bring glory' to Christ? In one sense, no; in another sense, yes; and in a third sense we merely behold his glory.

In terms of Christ's divine nature, he has a glory that cannot be added to or taken away. God's glory is an essential aspect of his nature. He is infinitely glorious and no creature can fully comprehend that glory, much less diminish it. We can call this Christ's essential glory. There is, however, a second glory that belongs only to the Son, and not to the Father or the Spirit, namely, the glory of the incarnation. This is the glory of Christ as the God-man, which we may call a personal glory. As the God-man, Jesus is the 'image of the invisible God' (Col. 1:15); 'He is the radiance of the glory of God and the exact imprint of his nature' (Heb. 1:3). John also speaks of Christ's personal glory, which he saw, 'glory as of the only Son from the Father' (John 1:14). The word glory is a word used to describe God's visible manifestation (Exod. 33:22). Thus in the Temple, where God's presence is peculiarly manifested, his people cry 'Glory' (Ps. 29:9). Christ replaces the Temple built by hands with his body so that he uniquely manifests God in a way that no building or other person can ever come close to (John 2:19–21). Christ's body (temple) was 'destroyed', but on the third day he was raised in power and glory (Rom. 1:4; 1 Cor. 15:35–49).

Before Christ was resurrected, the glory of his person was veiled to some extent. After all, Isaiah 53:2 affirms that Christ 'had no form or majesty that we should look at him, and no beauty that we should desire him.' In fact, men hid their faces from the Son, and despised him (Isa. 53:3). These words clearly have in view Christ's state of humiliation. However, in the accounts of Christ's transfiguration (Matt. 17), we have a glimpse into his personal glory, which was usually veiled during his earthly ministry. James, Peter and John had a special look at the glory of Christ, which resurrected saints will behold in heaven. At that moment there was a brief revelation of the divine, heavenly glory of Christ, which the saints on earth all long for as they live by faith, not by sight. The point is that the transfiguration was a prelude to the glorious bodily transformation that would take place at Christ's resurrection, and especially at his enthronement. From the time of his ascension and enthronement onwards the saints of God, when they see him face-to-face, will see the splendor of Christ's divine glory shining through his humanity.

This glory, then, belongs to Christ's person as the God-man. His incarnation, quite apart from his mediation on behalf of sinners, meant that he possessed a glory that was unique to him. This seems like an appropriate time to speak about a much-disputed issue in the church today, that is, pictures of Christ. Assuming we are willing to grant that Christ's appearance changed as he entered his state of exaltation, which I think is indisputable (Luke 24:31), are pictures of Christ a reflection of him in his state of humiliation or his state of exaltation? Surely we desire to behold the risen Jesus? But we must ask the question: Can we ever capture the glory of the exalted God-man in a picture? After all, his glory must necessarily transcend a picture because his glory is immaterial.

There is the added problem that if the picture represents Christ, as it purports to do, then why do we not worship the picture? The vision of Christ at the consummation will certainly cause us to fall down and worship him (see Phil. 2:9–11). If we do not worship the picture because it is not really Christ, then what is the point? Some

(?) When Ezekiel had a vision of the heavenly throne and saw the likeness of a man upon it, he could only describe what he saw as several steps removed from the reality—'the appearance of the likeness of the glory of the LORD' (Ezek. 1:26–8). Is it possible for pictures to faithfully represent the exalted Christ now seated in glory?

might respond that Jesus was seen by his disciples and thousands of other people during his life; but we must remember that they actually saw, even if it was not with the eyes of faith, the true Christ, not a representation of him. Worshipping him in that context would have been entirely appropriate. I offer these questions and comments in light of the basic argument of this book, which insists that Christ's human nature underwent development, from humiliation to glory. For Christians, the closest (and best) picture we have of Christ while pilgrims on earth is the elements of bread and wine given to us in the Lord's Supper—elements that we view by sight, but are ultimately only any use to us if received by faith.

There is also a third glory that belongs to Christ, which is connected with his personal glory: the glory of his mediatorial work. Christ is glorified not only because he is the God-man, but he is glorified because of what he does. That means he is glorified in his people (John 17:10). Humans cannot add to or take away from God's essential glory. But in the case of Christ's mediatorial glory, things are different. Hence in John 17 Christ prays that glory has come to him from his disciples. Not only Christ's disciples at that time, but all believers will bring glory to Christ and the Father (John 14:13). This has to do with his mediatorial work on their behalf.

His mediation is only for a time. This explains how at the end Christ can hand the kingdom over to his Father (1 Cor. 15:24). Christ's high priestly prayer in John 17—a picture of his intercession now in heaven—shows Christ asking for glory in order that he may glorify his Father (17:1–2). Verse 2 speaks of Christ's 'authority over all flesh', which he received from the Father. The authority Christ receives, dependent upon his death and resurrection (see Matt. 28:18), allows him to grant eternal life to his people. In verse 4 Christ claims to have glorified his Father by doing the work the Father gave him to do. Christ has in view here his impending death as well. The glory that Christ asks for in the presence of God no doubt includes his glorified humanity, but it also includes the reward that is due to him for his obedience to death on the cross, namely the salvation of the church (John 17:6ff.).

Because Christ's personal glory transcends the glory of his mediatorship, when he hands over the kingdom to his Father he will retain this personal glory. Thus while his offices of prophet, priest, and king will end at the consummation because the salvation of his bride and the destruction of his enemies are complete, his glory as Mediator remains. Indeed, his personal glory as the God-man means that he will rule his kingdom in the age to come (Heb. 2:5), thus retaining his kingship. As argued above, Christ will reveal the mind of God to the glorified saints in heaven, thus retaining his prophetic office. Lastly, Revelation 22:2 indicates that the 'tree of life' in heaven, that is for the 'healing of the nations', is a figurative picture of Christ's accomplished redemptive work; and thus Christ's priestly office will be remembered, even though his oblation and intercession are no longer needed. So we can say that the saving activity of Christ in his three offices ends at the consummation. However, that does not mean he no longer functions as prophet, priest, and king because his person as the God-man remains forever and ever. That is to say, the principle expressed in the office continues to have an abiding influence in heaven. It is the person of Christ that Christians will behold in glory, and that glorious hope brings us to our final consideration: the beatific vision.

BEATIFIC VISION

To behold God in Christ is to behold his glory; and the sight of this glory is something that saints on earth must long patiently for while they live by faith in the Son of God who loved them and gave himself for them.[29] In Christ alone we have the fullest and best view of the glory of God. There are two ways to behold the glory of God in the face of Jesus Christ: by faith and by sight. In this world Christians desire to see Christ face-to-face. This is why we long for heaven. But in this world Christ's sheep live by faith whereas in the world to come they will live by sight and so apprehend Christ visibly.

Bracelets with the letters WWJD ('What Would Jesus Do?') are common in Christian circles. This reflects the teaching of the medieval Catholic theologian, Thomas à Kempis (c. 1380–1471), whose book, *The Imitation of Christ*, remains popular even today. No one can criticize the attempt to be conformed to the image of Jesus (Rom. 8:29). Owen made a salient point in connection with this manner of thinking. He wrote: 'No man shall ever become 'like unto him' by bare imitation of his actions, without that view or intuition of his glory which alone is accompanied with a transforming power to change them into the same image.'[30] We are bound to fix our thoughts on Jesus (Heb. 3:1), both on his person and work. We would do better to ask, 'What Did Jesus Do?' ('WDJD') in order to motivate our obedience to him; but we do even better to meditate on his person as well.

As we live by faith in this world, we must ask ourselves whether we contemplate the glory of Christ's person and work. Indeed, our growth in grace may be discerned by answering that question. A true Christian is one in whose heart God has shone 'the light of the knowledge of the glory of God in the face of Jesus Christ' (2 Cor. 4:6). In Christ alone the glory of the invisible God shines forth. Our faith is directed towards Christ crucified, risen and ascended. Faith in Christ is the fountain of our evangelical obedience, for the just not only are justified by faith but live by faith (Rom. 1:17). In fact, the best privilege in this life is beholding Christ's glory by faith. To put it differently, only those who behold Christ by faith in this world will have the privilege of beholding him by sight in heaven.

In keeping with the basic argument of this book, the way in which we are to behold the glory of God in the person of Jesus Christ in this life is by first meditating on his person and then by meditating upon his work. The simple fact that the eternal Son of God, who is infinite, eternal, unchangeable, omnipotent, and omniscient (to name a few attributes), took on finite flesh should astound us. It no doubt stunned heaven into awed silence—though the angels sang at his birth! Because of the union of the two natures we have an access to God that would otherwise have been impossible. We have access to the knowledge of God through the Son of God. We have a brother who is Yahweh. But we are not only to contemplate his person; we must also meditate upon the fact that this person is our prophet, priest, and king. Thus, Paul keeps these two elements (Christ's person and work) in close connection when he speaks of his desire to know Christ Jesus and the power of his resurrection so that he may attain the resurrection of the dead, and so behold Christ (Phil. 3:10). Before that, however, Paul speaks in Philippians 2:5–11 about the person and work of Christ wherein the Son of God humbled himself and died an ignominious death, only to be raised to glory. In other words, Paul's grasp of the person and work of Christ and their connection (shown in Phil. 2) led him to the attitude of desiring to know Christ that we see in Philippians 3. These are the truths about Christ that Christians should meditate upon as they prepare themselves to enjoy God eternally through Jesus Christ.

Our heavenly enjoyment of the person of Christ will be by sight. This vision is a transforming vision; it changes us into the image of Christ. That seems to be the meaning of John's words in 1 John 3:2, 'Beloved, we are God's children now, and what we will be has not yet appeared; but we know that when he appears we shall be like him, because we shall see him as he is.' This may appear to be a radical statement, but we should remember that beholding the glory of God in this life by faith is the means by which we are transformed into the image of God. As Paul writes in 2 Corinthians 3:18, 'And we all, with unveiled face, beholding the glory of the Lord, are being transformed into the same image from one degree of glory to another.' So, just as a parent is 'transformed' by the sight of their missing child, or a student is 'transformed' when they first look at their acceptance letter to college, believers will be in a far more transcending manner utterly and perfectly transformed by the *sight* of the person of Jesus Christ in his regal glory.

The reason theologians have called the vision of Christ 'beatific' is because 'it gives perfect rest and blessedness unto them in whom it is.' So in heaven there will be, according to Owen, 'continual operations of God in Christ in the souls of them that are glorified, and communications from him unto them.'[31] If we are sustained daily by God's grace to our souls in this life, then surely in the life to come we will experience this to an even greater degree. For that reason we can be sure that just as revelation now comes through Christ to the church, so in glory it will be the same. There is continuity in terms of God's dealings with his people between this world and the world to come, even though we move from our own state of humiliation to exaltation.

(?) Heaven has many glories, but what will be the greatest glory that believers will see? Will we see anything more glorious than the sight of Jesus Christ in the flesh?

As the incarnate Son, Christ will forever perform the function of mediator between humanity and God. That is a privilege that belongs to him on account of his personal glory. His mediatorial glory means, of course, that he will not be alone in heaven. Indeed, because God hates divorce (Mal. 2:16), and because we are married to Christ (Eph. 5:25–7; Rev. 21:2), our eternal enjoyment of God in the person of Jesus Christ is guaranteed. Heaven's eternity for believers is grounded in our union with the God-man who, in his ascended, glorified humanity, lives forever. Because we are married to Christ we have the right to behold him forever by sight. In the words of Job 19:25–6:

> For I know that my Redeemer lives,
> and at the last he will stand upon the earth.
> And after my skin has been thus destroyed,
> yet in my flesh I shall see God.

Job's hope and desire are salutary reminders to Christians of how we ought to hope. Our hope consists of this: that as 'a man sees his neighbor when they stand and converse together face to face, so shall we see the Lord Christ in his glory.' This is the immediate sight of Christ that Christians in this life 'do breathe and pant after'.[32] Do you?

CONCLUDING THOUGHTS

The Dutch theologian, G. C. Berkouwer, correctly notes that in the Scriptures 'we continually encounter the irrefragable unity of Christ's person and work…Not to know who he is means: not to understand what his work is; and not to see his work in the right perspective is not to understand his person.'[33] This book is designed to be a primer on Christology, and for that reason it necessarily looks at Christ's person and work. The emphasis on his person has been deliberate, if only to help us better appreciate his work for us.

The doctrine of justification by faith depends on Christ's perfect and complete obedience to the law of God, as well as his sacrificial death on the cross, in our place. The above has demonstrated, I hope, that Christ's obedience was not, to use a colloquial phrase, 'a mere walk in the park'. He was the man who lived by faith during his life on earth; he is the man who was tempted in every way that we are; and he is the man who now reigns in heaven as the Lord of heaven and earth. So we are commanded to look to Jesus, 'the founder and perfecter of our faith, who for the joy that was set before him endured the cross, despising the shame, and is seated at the right hand of the throne of God' (Heb. 12:1–2). When we pray we are assured that the Spirit prays in us (Rom. 8:26–7) because Christ intercedes for us (Heb. 7:25). Our prayers rise up to God on the wings of faith because Christ bridges the gap between a holy God and sinful humanity. Let us not forget that our prayer life is only possible because 'In the days of his flesh, Jesus offered up prayers and supplications, with loud cries and tears, to him who was able to save him from death' (Heb. 5:7). Whatever Christ merited for us he possessed in himself first, including faith, love, hope, election, justification, sanctification, adoption, and glorification.

In his fascinating study on Cyril of Alexandria, John A. McGuckin notes the following premise of Cyril's: 'that in christology the implications are crucial to the argument.'[34] How we conceive of Christ's person, and the relation between the two natures, will have a profound impact on how we understand his work. It cannot be otherwise. Moreover, whether we love Christ's person is an indicator of whether we really love his work. It is one thing to love the benefits, but it seems as though we cannot love the benefits without loving the author of them. We are in no position to treat Christ as though he were a prostitute by taking from him some personal benefit without any real love for his person. If we love him now by faith our natural desire is to be with him forever, to gaze upon the 'most handsome of the sons of men' (Ps. 45:2) in the glorified beauty of his being, thus enjoying the blessed vision of the one who is chief among ten thousand. Little wonder that so many great theologians spoke of the precedence of his person over his work. Perhaps that precedence is why we can understand the sentiment echoed by some that Christ did not come into the world for us, but we for Christ.

Sinners who wish to be saved by the Savior must confess that his humanity is as important as his divinity. This confession leads us to the conclusion that the person of Christ is absolutely vital for our salvation, and that we are commanded by God's word to know him who was sent by the Father. As Warfield notes, we must know him not as 'a humanized God or a deified man, but a true God-man—one who is all that God is and at the same time all that man is: on whose almighty arm we can rest, and to whose human sympathy we can appeal. We cannot afford to lose either the God in the man or the man in the God; our hearts cry out for the complete God-man whom the Scriptures offer us.'[35] And this gaze is ours to behold one day by sight; but until then we must behold the glory of Christ by faith.

ENDNOTES

1   *Exposition of Hebrews*, XIX.37 in *The Works of John Owen, D.D.* 24 vols. (Edinburgh: Johnstone & Hunter, 1850–53); *John Calvin: Institutes of Christian Religion*. Ed. John T. McNeil. Trans. Ford Lewis Battles. (Philadelphia: Westminster Press, 1960), II.xii.4–5.

2   *Exposition of Ephesians*, I.99 in *The Works of Thomas Goodwin, D.D.* 12 vols. (Grand Rapids: Reformation Heritage Books, 2006).

3   *Exposition of Ephesians*, I.100.

4   *Discourses Upon the Existence and attributes of God* (London, 1840), 574.

5   Ep. 202, to Nectarius in NPNF2, v. 7.

6   *Existence and attributes*, 436.

7   In my view, if ever a theologian has been unfairly represented and badly understood it was Nestorius.

8   *Reformed Dogmatics: Sin and Salvation in Christ*, vol. 3 (Grand Rapids: Baker, 2006), 256.

9   Ibid.

10   Ibid., 257.

11   *Person of Christ* (Downers Grove: InterVarsity Press, 1998), 226.

12   Quoted in Macleod, *Person of Christ*, 230.

13   Iain Murray, *The Life of John Murray* (Edinburgh: The Banner of Truth Trust, 2007), 211–12.

14   *Christ the Mediator*, V.143.

15   Ibid.

16   Christopher Wright, *Knowing Jesus through the Old Testament* (Downer's Grove: IVP, 1992), 108.

17   *Reformed Dogmatics*, III.309.

18   *Looking Unto Jesus: A View of the Everlasting Gospel* […] (Pittsburgh: Luke Loomis & Co., 1882), 514.

19   *Works, Pneumatologia*, III.160.

20   Ibid., 162.

21   *The Holy Spirit* (Downers Grove: InterVarsity Press, 1996), 38.

22   The Holy Spirit, 53.

23   John Owen, *The Holy Spirit* (Fearn: Christian Heritage, 2004) 132.

24   *Reformed Dogmatics*, III.292.

25   *The Complete Works of Thomas Manton*. 22 vols. (London: James Nisbet, 1870), X.123.

26   *Meditations and Discourses on the Glory of Christ,* 1.414.

27   *Exposition of Ephesians*, II.162.

28   I am thankful for Edward Reynolds' thoughts on this, which are found in his work, an explication of the Hundred and Tenth Psalm (London, 1837), 6–7.

29   In this section I am indebted to John Owen's excellent treatise on the beatific vision in *Meditations and Discourses on The Glory of Christ*, 1.302ff.

30   Ibid., 304.

31   Ibid., 413.

32   Ibid., 379.

33   *The Person of Christ*, (Grand Rapids: Eerdmans, 1954), 105.

34   *Saint Cyril of Alexandria and the Christological Controversy* (New York: St. Vladimir's Seminary Press, 2004), 129.

35   B. B. Warfield, *Selected Shorter Writings*, Vol. I (New Jersey: P&R, 1972), 166.

SUGGESTIONS FOR FURTHER READING

Fine works on the early Christological debates:

McGuckin, John A. *St. Cyril of Alexandria: The Christological Controversy: Its History, Theology, and Texts*. Crestwood, N.Y.: St. Vladimir's Seminary Press, 2004.

Wessel, Susan. *Cyril of Alexandria and the Nestorian Controversy: The Making of a Saint and of a Heretic*. Oxford: Oxford University Press, 2004.

Reformation and Post-Reformation Christology:

Jones, Mark. *Why Heaven Kissed Earth: the Christology of the Puritan Reformed Orthodox theologian, Thomas Goodwin (1600–1680)*. Göttingen: Vandenhoeck & Ruprecht, 2010.

Spence, Alan. *Incarnation and Inspiration John Owen and the Coherence of Christology.* London: T & T Clark, 2007.

Willis, Edward David. *Calvin's Catholic Christology. The Function of the so-Called Extra Calvinisticum in Calvin's Theology.* Leiden: E.J. Brill, 1967.

Modern treatments on Christology worth consulting:

Macleod, Donald. *The Person of Christ.* Downers Grove, Ill: InterVarsity Press, 1998.

Macleod, Donald. *From Glory to Golgotha: Controversial Issues in the Life of Christ.* Fearn: Christian Focus, 2002.

Warfield, Benjamin Breckinridge. *The Person and Work of Christ.* Philadelphia, Pa: Presbyterian and Reformed Pub. Co, 1950.

See especially Warfield's excellent essay, "The Emotional Life of Our Lord", which can be found at: www.monergism.com/thethreshold/articles/onsite/emotionallife.html

For combining good Christology and devotion, the following Puritan works are indispensable:

Ambrose, Isaac. *Looking Unto Jesus: A View of the Everlasting Gospel.* Pittsburgh: Luke Loomis & Co., 1882. (Can be accessed on google books)

Goodwin, Thomas. *Christ Set Forth & The Heart of Christ in Heaven Towards Sinners on Earth.* Ross-shire, Scotland: Christian Focus, 2011.

Owen, John. *The Glory of Christ.* Fearn: Christian Heritage, 2004.

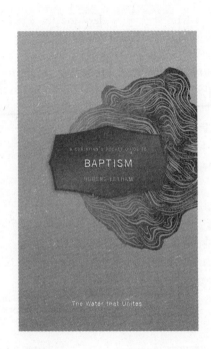

A CHRISTIAN'S POCKET GUIDE TO

BAPTISM

ROBERT LETHAM

The Water that Unites